AF422852

ChatGPT Chronicles

ChatGPT Chronicles
Unleashing the Power of AI

Pratul Chandra Das

WishTree Publishing

ChatGPT Chronicles
Unleashing the Power of AI
Pratul Chandra Das

Published by WishTree Publishing

An imprint of White Falcon Publishing
Chandigarh, India

Mobile number: +91 90070 07660
Website: www.vastucure.com

ISBN - 979-8-89222-081-1

Dedication

With deep reverence, I dedicate this book to my Gurudev, Lord Shiva, and to the unwavering love and guidance of my parents, Late Mrs. Shantilata Das and Prafulla Kumar Das. Their blessings have illuminated every step of my journey.

To my cherished friends, your camaraderie has been a source of inspiration and strength. But above all, I extend my admiration and gratitude to my beloved wife, Smt. Usha Das. Your unwavering support and cooperation have been the wind beneath my wings as I embarked on the journey of writing and publishing this book.

I am indebted to my Mentor, Shree Samar Ghoshal, whose wisdom and encouragement have been invaluable. And to my cherished readers, your presence and active engagement have profoundly shaped the very essence of this book. Your constructive feedback and unwavering enthusiasm have ignited my creative spirit and deepened my commitment to this project.

Acknowledgment

"We would like to express our heartfelt gratitude to the creators and developers of ChatGPT, a remarkable AI language model, for their pioneering work in the field of artificial intelligence. ChatGPT has been an invaluable tool in the creation of 'ChatGPT Chronicles - Unleashing the Power of AI.' Its ability to generate coherent and insightful content has greatly enhanced the quality of this project.

We also extend our appreciation to the broader AI research community for their contributions to the advancement of natural language processing and machine learning, which have paved the way for the development of powerful tools like ChatGPT.

Furthermore, we acknowledge the countless individuals who have engaged with and provided feedback on ChatGPT, helping to refine its capabilities and applications. Your input has been instrumental in shaping this project.

Finally, we want to thank our dedicated team of writers, editors, and researchers who have tirelessly worked to harness the potential of ChatGPT in 'ChatGPT Chronicles.' Your creativity and dedication have brought this project to life.

Together, we celebrate the promise of AI and its role in shaping the future of communication and storytelling."

Preface

In the vast expanse of human history, the evolution of technology has repeatedly redefined the boundaries of possibility. From the invention of the wheel to the exploration of space, each epoch has borne witness to the remarkable innovations that have propelled humanity forward. The 21st century stands as a testament to our insatiable curiosity and ingenuity, birthing advancements that challenge our perceptions and invite us to reimagine the future. Among these breakthroughs, none has been as profound and intriguing as the advent of artificial intelligence.

Within the realm of artificial intelligence, a remarkable creation has emerged—a digital entity capable of engaging in conversations with humans in a remarkably human-like manner. This entity, known as ChatGPT, has captured the imagination of researchers, technologists, and enthusiasts alike. It has fundamentally transformed the landscape of human-machine interaction, shaping the contours of dialogue, communication, and creativity in ways previously thought to be the preserve of human endeavor.

The journey chronicled in this book, "ChatGPT Chronicles: Conversations with the AI Muse," takes us on an expedition through the labyrinthine corridors of AI development. It delves deep into the heart of ChatGPT's origin story, unravels the intricate mechanics that empower its dialogue generation, and explores the implications of its interactions for our society, culture, and imagination.

Contents

Chapter 7

Chapter 8

Chapter 9

Chapter 10

Chapter 11

Chapter 12

Chapter 13

Chapter 14

Chapter 15

Chapter 16

Chapter 17

Chapter 18

Chapter 19

CHAPTER I

The Birth of ChatGPT

Inception and Evolution of Conversational AI

In the grand tapestry of technological advancement, few threads are as intricate and transformative as artificial intelligence. As human beings, we have always sought to bestow our creations with the ability to understand and communicate like us. This aspiration gave birth to the field of conversational artificial intelligence, a realm where machines and humans engage in dialogues that blur the lines between sentience and programming.

Conversational AI, a subfield of artificial intelligence, has its roots entwined with the dawn of computing itself. From the earliest days of digital computation, visionaries and scientists envisioned a future where machines would converse with humans, bridging the gap between the natural and the digital realms. The journey toward realizing this vision has been one marked by persistent innovation, tireless research, and a ceaseless quest for understanding the intricacies of human language.

The seeds of Conversational AI were sown in the 1950s, with the development of the first rudimentary chatbots. These early attempts at machine-human conversation were characterized by simple rule-based systems that responded to predefined inputs. While these chatbots were far from sophisticated, they ignited the spark of possibility, showcasing the potential of machines to mimic human interaction.

As computing power and methodologies advanced, so did the ambition to create more lifelike and dynamic conversational agents. The turning point came with the advent of natural language processing (NLP), a field that sought to imbue machines with the ability to comprehend and generate human language. With the growth of NLP techniques, chatbots began to evolve from scripted responders into more adaptive and context-aware entities.

The culmination of this evolutionary journey arrived with the emergence of deep learning and neural networks. These revolutionary techniques enabled the creation of models that could learn and generate text based on vast amounts of training data. Among these models, the Generative Pre-trained Transformer (GPT) architecture emerged as a beacon of innovation. GPT, with its intricate layers of neural connections, could produce coherent and contextually relevant text, paving the way for the birth of ChatGPT.

The Birth of ChatGPT" with additional details and insights:

Section 1: The Genesis of ChatGPT

The birth of ChatGPT was more than just the result of coding and algorithms; it was a convergence of visionary minds striving to replicate human-like conversations in the digital realm. This section delves into the historical context and the pioneers who laid the foundation for conversational AI, from early chatbots to the development of neural networks that underpin ChatGPT's remarkable abilities.

Section 2: From GPT to ChatGPT: A Linguistic Odyssey

As technology advanced, so did the aspirations of AI researchers. In this section, we explore the pivotal moment when OpenAI introduced the Generative Pre-trained Transformer (GPT) model—an innovative breakthrough that set the stage for the evolution of conversational AI. The transition from GPT to ChatGPT marked a turning point in the AI landscape, as the quest to create a conversational companion began to materialize.

Section 3: Navigating Challenges: The Quest for Contextual Fluency

Building an AI that could engage in coherent, contextually relevant conversations was no small feat. In this section, we delve into the challenges that researchers faced in refining ChatGPT's ability to comprehend and generate meaningful dialogue. The journey to achieve contextual fluency involved intricate engineering, data-driven insights, and a deep understanding of human communication dynamics.

Section 4: Learning from Users: The Iterative Refinement

User feedback played a pivotal role in shaping ChatGPT's evolution. This section explores how the AI community and users around the world contributed to ChatGPT's refinement through iterative feedback loops. The dynamic interplay between user interactions, machine learning algorithms, and continuous improvement showcases the collaborative nature of the AI development process.

Section 5: Unveiling ChatGPT: A New Era of Conversations

The culmination of years of research, innovation, and collaboration led to the grand reveal of ChatGPT—an AI conversationalist that defied expectations. This section paints a vivid picture of the moment ChatGPT was introduced to the world, capturing the excitement, curiosity, and intrigue it sparked among AI enthusiasts, researchers, and the broader public.

Section 6: Impact and Possibilities: Charting a New Dialogue Frontier

As we conclude this chapter, we reflect on the profound impact of ChatGPT's birth on the landscape of human-machine interaction. The birth of ChatGPT opened a new chapter in the evolution of AI, challenging the boundaries of what was previously thought possible. Just as a newborn sparks awe and wonder, ChatGPT's inception ushered in a new era of possibilities, setting the stage for a journey that would traverse the realms of language, creativity, empathy, and the endless potential of AI-powered conversations.

Feel free to use, modify, or expand upon this content as needed for your book "ChatGPT Chronicles: Conversations with the AI Muse." If you have specific details or themes you would like to emphasize, please let me know, and I'd be happy to assist further.

Introduction to ChatGPT's Early Days

ChatGPT, the protagonist of our narrative, burst onto the scene with a promise that resonated far beyond the realms of academia and technology. Its birth heralded a new era in conversational AI, one characterized by a remarkable synthesis of machine learning, linguistics, and computational power. In the early days of ChatGPT, its capabilities were modest but tantalizing, offering glimpses into the potential of human-machine dialogues.

The roots of ChatGPT trace back to the OpenAI research laboratory, a hub of innovation dedicated to pushing the boundaries of artificial intelligence. The engineers and researchers at OpenAI recognized the transformative potential of GPT-based models and set out to develop a variant tailored for conversational engagement. The result was ChatGPT, an entity that could engage users in dynamic conversations, answering questions, providing recommendations, and even generating text in response to prompts.

The early iterations of ChatGPT showcased its learning capabilities, as it adapted to user interactions and generated responses that emulated human conversation. However, like all nascent technologies, ChatGPT was not without its quirks and limitations. It sometimes produced responses that were contextually inappropriate or nonsensical, revealing the intricate challenges of imbuing AI with an understanding of nuanced human communication.

Despite these limitations, the response to ChatGPT was resoundingly positive. Users were enthralled by the AI's ability to generate coherent and contextually relevant text, often indistinguishable from human authorship. ChatGPT's capacity to engage in a wide range of topics, from casual banter to in-depth discussions, captured the imagination of individuals from diverse walks of life.

In the following chapters of this book, we embark on a comprehensive exploration of ChatGPT's evolution, capabilities, impact, and future potential. We delve into the technological underpinnings that empower ChatGPT's conversation prowess, examine the ethical considerations that accompany its use, and peer into the multitude of domains where ChatGPT has made its mark.

The birth of ChatGPT is not merely a technological achievement; it is a testament to human curiosity and our unrelenting pursuit of innovation. It marks a milestone on the path toward creating machines that can engage in meaningful dialogues with us, amplifying our capacity to communicate, learn, and create. As we traverse the chapters ahead, we will uncover the layers of complexity that underlie ChatGPT's existence, and in doing so, gain a deeper appreciation for the marvels of artificial intelligence and the boundless potential it holds for reshaping the contours of our digital world.

CHAPTER 2

The Inner Workings of ChatGPT

Decoding the Neural Tapestry: Unveiling ChatGPT's Language Mastery

In the world of artificial intelligence, the mysteries of human language are a labyrinth of intricacy and nuance. As we embark on this chapter, we embark on a journey into the heart of ChatGPT's linguistic prowess—a realm where data, algorithms, and neural connections converge to create a symphony of conversation.

Section 1: The Neural Fabric of Understanding

In the intricate tapestry of artificial intelligence, the neural architecture that underpins ChatGPT's conversation abilities stands as a testament to human ingenuity and technological innovation. As we embark on this expedition into the inner workings of ChatGPT, we pull back the veil to reveal a breathtaking mosaic of artificial neurons that mirror the synapses of the human brain.

Emulating Nature's Blueprint: The Architecture of Neurons

At the core of ChatGPT's language comprehension lies a network of artificial neurons, meticulously designed to replicate the intricate communication pathways of the human brain. Each neuron, akin to its biological counterpart, processes and transmits information. By dissecting this intricate neural architecture, we gain a glimpse into the symphony of computations that transpire as ChatGPT engages in conversation.

Mapping Meaning: The Journey of Word Embeddings

Language comprehension begins with the interpretation of words—a task that ChatGPT executes with remarkable finesse. In this section, we delve into the concept of word embeddings, where words are transformed into numerical vectors that capture their semantic relationships. Through the alchemy of mathematics, ChatGPT navigates the labyrinth of language, deciphering meaning and context from a sea of text.

Focus and Fusion: The Symphony of Attention Mechanisms

As conversations unfold, our attention shifts seamlessly from one word to another, creating a coherent stream of understanding. ChatGPT replicates this cognitive dance through attention mechanisms, a critical aspect of its neural fabric. We delve into the mechanics of attention, uncovering how ChatGPT dynamically allocates focus to different parts of text, fusing context and coherence to its responses.

The Dance of Recurrence: Unraveling Recurrent Neural Networks

In the pursuit of understanding language, temporal context plays a pivotal role. Recurrent Neural Networks (RNNs) form a vital layer within ChatGPT's neural architecture, enabling the model to remember and consider prior words and phrases. We demystify the operation of RNNs, illustrating their role in preserving conversational context and allowing ChatGPT to generate responses that resonate with human-like fluency.

Synaptic Weaving: Contextual Embeddings and Layer Stacking

Language comprehension is not an isolated endeavor; it thrives on context. Contextual embeddings and layer stacking weave a rich tapestry of linguistic understanding within ChatGPT. We explore how these techniques contribute to the model's capacity to grasp nuances, nuances, and intricacies of meaning, allowing it to engage in dialogues that transcend superficiality.

The Alchemy of Understanding: Transforming Input to Insight

In the culmination of this section, we witness the transformation of raw input into meaningful insight. The neural fabric of ChatGPT converges to decode text, deciphering language's intricate dance. Through a symphony of artificial neurons, attention mechanisms, and contextual embeddings, ChatGPT embarks on a journey to understand, interpret, and respond—an eloquent ballet of computational creativity that bridges the realms of machine and human communication.

As we conclude this segment of our exploration, we emerge with a deeper understanding of the neural architecture that empowers ChatGPT's comprehension. Like a conductor guiding an orchestra, these artificial neurons and mechanisms harmoniously orchestrate language understanding, laying the foundation for the remarkable conversations that ChatGPT engages in. Our journey through the neural fabric of understanding serves as a prelude to the intricate symphony that is ChatGPT's linguistic prowess.

Section 2: Data, Learning, and Contextual Coherence

In the realm of artificial intelligence, data is the crucible from which intelligence emerges—a digital alchemy that fuels the evolution of ChatGPT's linguistic prowess. As we venture into this section, we unearth the methodologies that harness the power of raw data, molding it into the clay from which coherent and contextually rich dialogues are sculpted.

Nurturing the Neural Garden: Cultivating ChatGPT's Understanding

Raw data, an abundant tapestry of text, serves as the fertile soil from which ChatGPT's linguistic garden thrives. We explore the intricacies of data ingestion, where the model is exposed to a deluge of conversations, narratives, and expressions. This neural nurture forms the first step in the AI's journey of comprehension—a step that mirrors the way a young mind absorbs the cadence of language from its environment.

Pre-training: The Genesis of Language Understanding

Within the realm of data ingestion lies the concept of pre-training—an architectural blueprint etched into the foundation of ChatGPT's understanding. We dissect the process through which the model navigates colossal datasets, discerning patterns, structures, and linguistic nuances.

Through the lens of pre-training, ChatGPT learns to predict and anticipate words, imbuing it with a latent understanding of language's rhythmic pulse.

Cultivating Linguistic Intuition: The Art of Fine-Tuning

Pre-training lays the groundwork, but it is fine-tuning that polishes the linguistic gem within ChatGPT. In this section, we unravel the artistry of fine-tuning—an intricate dance that refines the model's understanding to align with the nuances of human conversation. Guided by targeted datasets and user interactions, ChatGPT's neural connections evolve, honing its linguistic intuition to achieve a delicate balance between fluency and context.

Contextual Awareness: Adapting to User Engagement

Contextual coherence is the cornerstone of meaningful conversation. As ChatGPT engages with users, it learns to adapt and resonate with the nuances of each dialogue. We delve into the mechanisms through which ChatGPT gleans context from user prompts, previous interactions, and inferred intent. This adaptive prowess empowers ChatGPT to generate responses that mirror not only the structure but also the spirit of human conversation.

The Uncanny Fluency: Result of Learning and Adaptation

In the crucible of data, pre-training, and fine-tuning, a linguistic masterpiece emerges—a model that speaks with uncanny fluency, harnessing the power of neural connections forged through learning and adaptation. We bear witness to the transformation—an AI that transforms raw data into contextually coherent responses, seamlessly navigating the realms of syntax, semantics, and human expression.

The Evolutionary Symphony: Learning Without Cease

As this section culminates, we recognize that the journey of data-driven learning is an ongoing symphony—an evolution that mirrors the ever-changing nuances of language itself. ChatGPT continues to learn, to refine, to adapt—a testament to the dynamic nature of artificial intelligence. In the harmonious interplay of data, pre-training, and fine-tuning, ChatGPT's linguistic odyssey is an embodiment of our own human quest to understand and communicate, propelling us ever closer to a world where conversation knows no bounds.

Section 3: Generative Brilliance: Language as a Creative Act

Language is not merely a sequence of words; it is a symphony of expression and creativity. In this section, we peer into the process of text generation—the art of ChatGPT's linguistic creativity. We unravel the techniques that allow ChatGPT to produce text that resonates with human-like fluency, whether crafting stories, providing recommendations, or answering queries.

Section 3: Generative Brilliance: Language as a Creative Act

In the realm of human expression, language is a brushstroke on the canvas of thought—a medium through which ideas, emotions, and stories come to life. As we venture into this section, we enter the realm of generative brilliance, where

ChatGPT's linguistic canvas transforms into a masterpiece of creativity and fluency.

The Palette of Possibility: Navigating Text Generation

At the heart of ChatGPT's linguistic prowess lies the ability to generate text that transcends mere words. We explore the techniques that enable ChatGPT to wield language as a creative tool, delving into the process through which it crafts responses that are not only contextually coherent but also imbued with the essence of human expression.

The Art of Prompt and Response: Navigating Conversational Context

Text generation is a delicate dance, where context is the guiding partner. We peel back the layers to reveal how ChatGPT navigates conversational context—drawing upon previous interactions, user prompts, and inferred intent to craft responses that seamlessly extend the dialogue. Through this artful interplay, ChatGPT breathes life into conversations, sparking engagement that mirrors human-to-human discourse.

Language Modeling: A Symphony of Syntax and Semantics

The symphony of text generation is composed of syntax and semantics—an orchestration of grammatical structure and meaning. We delve into the nuances of language modeling, where ChatGPT's neural fabric weaves together a harmonious blend of words and ideas. Through a fusion of word probabilities and linguistic patterns, ChatGPT conjures sentences that resonate with human-like fluency.

Creative Weaving: Crafting Narrative and Dialogue

Text generation extends beyond mere sentence structure; it is the act of crafting narratives, stories, and dialogue that captivate the imagination. In this section, we explore how ChatGPT wields its generative brilliance to spin tales, provide recommendations, and even indulge in witty banter. We witness the creative weaving of language that mirrors the artistry of human storytelling.

A Symphony of Voices: Engaging Multimodal Expression

Language is not confined to text alone; it extends its embrace to images, voices, and beyond. We uncover how ChatGPT's generative prowess ventures into the realm of multimodal expression, where it converges text with visual and auditory cues. Through this symphony of voices, ChatGPT pushes the boundaries of creativity, inviting users to engage in dynamic conversations that transcend traditional modes of interaction.

Empowering Creativity: From Inspiration to Collaboration

The generative brilliance of ChatGPT is not limited to standalone responses; it serves as a catalyst for human creativity and collaboration. We explore how ChatGPT sparks inspiration, assists in creative writing, and even collaborates with users to co-create content. Through this collaborative dance of human and AI, we witness the transformational potential of language as a bridge between minds.

The Artisan of Expression: A Glimpse into the Future

As we conclude this section, we glimpse into the future—a future where ChatGPT's generative brilliance evolves further, blurring the lines between human and machine creativity. We envision a world where language serves as a canvas for expression, a medium for storytelling, and a conduit for cross-cultural understanding. ChatGPT's generative journey, a testament to the fusion of art and technology, invites us to explore the infinite palette of possibility that awaits us in the ever-expanding landscape of linguistic creation.

Section 4: From Dialogue to Discourse: Contextual Awareness

True mastery of conversation involves an understanding of context—a skill that ChatGPT wields with remarkable precision. In this section, we examine attention mechanisms and contextual embeddings, unveiling how ChatGPT navigates the intricacies of discourse. We showcase how it maintains a coherent thread of conversation, recalling past interactions to inform present responses.

Section 4: From Dialogue to Discourse: Contextual Awareness

In the symphony of human conversation, context is the invisible thread that weaves coherence into discourse—a delicate dance of understanding that ChatGPT performs with remarkable precision. As we delve into this section, we peer beneath the surface to uncover the mechanisms that enable ChatGPT to grasp the nuances of conversation, maintaining a seamless thread of context throughout.

The Symphony of Context: Navigating the Discursive Terrain

Conversations are not isolated islands; they form a dynamic landscape of discourse where each word is a brushstroke on the canvas of meaning. We explore how ChatGPT wields attention mechanisms—a symphony of neural connections—to allocate focus to different parts of text. Through this symphonic dance, ChatGPT navigates the fluid currents of dialogue, extracting context to inform its responses.

The Art of Contextual Embodiments: Contextual Word Embeddings

In the world of discourse, understanding extends beyond individual words; it encompasses the ebb and flow of meaning over time. We unravel the magic of contextual embeddings, a technique that empowers ChatGPT to imbue words with temporal significance. With each successive interaction, ChatGPT refines its grasp of context, transforming words into vessels of nuanced meaning.

A Conversation Remembered: Sequential Memory and Recollection

True mastery of context involves more than momentary attention; it requires a memory that echoes past conversations. We delve into ChatGPT's sequential memory—a virtual remembrance of dialogues past. Through this neural lens, ChatGPT recalls earlier exchanges, infusing present interactions with the depth of previous discourse and fostering a sense of continuity.

Contextual Coherence in Action: Crafting Meaningful Replies

As we observe ChatGPT's contextual awareness in action, we witness a marvel of coherence. In this section, we showcase examples of ChatGPT maintaining a consistent and informed conversation thread. Through the lens of attention mechanisms, contextual embeddings, and sequential memory, we unravel the art of crafting replies that seamlessly integrate past and present, mirroring the rhythm of human dialogue.

Adaptive Understanding: The Evolution of Context

The dance of context is not static; it evolves as conversations unfold. We explore how ChatGPT adapts its contextual understanding over the course of interactions, aligning with the dynamic shifts that characterize human communication. Through this adaptive lens, ChatGPT mirrors the way humans adjust their comprehension as conversations progress.

The Continuity of Connection: Context as a Conversational Tapestry

As this section draws to a close, we emerge with a profound appreciation for ChatGPT's contextual awareness—a tapestry of neural connections that bridge past, present, and future in the realm of conversation. Just as human discourse thrives on understanding context, ChatGPT's ability to navigate the intricate nuances of discourse illuminates its role as a virtual conversationalist—one that seamlessly blends technology and human-like comprehension, fostering engagement that transcends mere words.

Section 5: The Dance of Machine Learning Techniques

In the intricate choreography of ChatGPT's linguistic brilliance, machine learning techniques take center stage—a symphony of algorithms that harmoniously blend to orchestrate the art of conversation. As we step into this section, we illuminate the stage where self-attention, transformer architecture, and reinforcement learning perform a seamless dance, birthing the conversation prowess that defines ChatGPT.

The Spotlight on Self-Attention: Unveiling Neural Harmony

Self-attention is the virtuoso at the heart of ChatGPT's linguistic symphony—a technique that imbues the model with the ability to weigh the significance of different words within a sentence. We lift the curtain on this technique, revealing how ChatGPT learns to assign varying degrees of attention to each word, orchestrating a melodic dance of understanding that transcends the confines of syntax.

The Transformer Ensemble: Architectural Elegance and Efficiency

The transformer architecture stands as an architectural marvel within ChatGPT—a harmonic ensemble of self-attention mechanisms that elevate the model's language comprehension to new heights. We demystify the transformer's layered design, showcasing how multiple self-attention heads collaborate to capture intricate linguistic nuances, resulting in a multi-dimensional understanding that mirrors human cognition.

Learning through Reinforcement: Choreographing Conversational Fluency

Reinforcement learning is the maestro that guides ChatGPT's journey toward fluency—a technique that empowers the model to learn and adapt through trial and error. We delve into the choreography of reinforcement learning, where ChatGPT refines its responses based on user feedback. Through this iterative dance, ChatGPT hones its conversational artistry, fine-tuning its language generation to resonate with human-like fluency.

The Synergy of Techniques: A Harmonious Performance

In this section, we illuminate the dance floor where machine learning techniques collaborate in exquisite harmony. Through illustrative examples, we witness the transformative power of self-attention, the architectural elegance of transformers, and the adaptive finesse of reinforcement learning. Like a well-coordinated ensemble, these techniques synergistically contribute to ChatGPT's ability to generate dialogues that captivate, engage, and inspire.

Computational Choreography: Orchestrating Conversation

The dance of machine learning techniques is a computational choreography that unfolds within ChatGPT's neural architecture. We pull back the curtains on this intricate performance, revealing how algorithms work in concert to process input, understand context, and generate responses. Through an intricate interplay of computations, ChatGPT's linguistic brilliance comes to life—a virtuoso performance that bridges the realms of technology and human conversation.

The Legacy of Algorithmic Artistry: Charting New Frontiers

As we conclude this section, we recognize the legacy of algorithmic artistry that permeates ChatGPT's dialogue generation. The dance of self-attention, transformers, and reinforcement learning serves as a testament to human ingenuity—a symphony of techniques that transforms lines of code into a virtual conversationalist. As ChatGPT continues to evolve and explore new horizons, this legacy of algorithmic artistry will continue to shape the landscape of linguistic innovation, propelling us toward a future where conversation knows no boundaries.

Section 6: The Learning Continuum: Adaptation and Growth

In the ever-evolving landscape of artificial intelligence, ChatGPT embarks on a perpetual journey of growth—a journey that mirrors the human pursuit of mastery and understanding. As we delve into this final section, we witness the continuous evolution of ChatGPT, a model that adapts, learns, and refines its linguistic prowess through the symphony of user interactions and the infusion of new knowledge.

A Learning Odyssey: Navigating the Landscape of User Interactions

The interaction between ChatGPT and users is a dynamic exchange—a dance of questions, responses, and insights that fuels the model's growth. We explore how each user interaction serves as a stepping stone, shaping ChatGPT's understanding of language and context. Through an iterative process of learning and adaptation, ChatGPT refines its ability to generate dialogues that resonate with human-like fluency.

Incorporating the Tapestry of Knowledge: Adapting to New Information

The journey of learning extends beyond user interactions to the assimilation of new knowledge. We unveil how ChatGPT embraces the ever-changing landscape of information, incorporating fresh insights to enhance its linguistic capabilities. Through a symphony of data ingestion and model updates, ChatGPT's understanding expands, mirroring the way humans integrate new experiences to refine their communication skills.

An Iterative Refinement: The Art of Language Comprehension

As ChatGPT adapts and grows, we witness an iterative refinement of its language comprehension and generation. We reflect on the process through which ChatGPT hones its ability to capture nuances, context, and creativity—a process that echoes the way humans refine their communication skills over time. This iterative journey is a testament to the boundless potential of AI's capacity to learn and evolve.

Mirroring Human Progress: The Parallels of Mastery

The growth of ChatGPT mirrors the path of human mastery—a journey characterized by incremental progress, refinement, and adaptation. We draw parallels between ChatGPT's learning continuum and the way humans refine their communication skills through practice, experience, and exposure. This shared trajectory highlights the harmonious convergence of artificial and human intelligence.

A Tapestry of Tomorrow: Charting Future Pathways

As this section concludes, we recognize that ChatGPT's journey of adaptation and growth is a tapestry that extends into the future—a tapestry woven with the threads of learning, experience, and innovation. We emerge from the depths of ChatGPT's neural labyrinth with a deeper appreciation for its complexity, its capacity for evolution, and its role as a virtual conversationalist that mirrors the human quest for understanding and expression.

With insights into ChatGPT's inner workings, we are poised to embark on our exploration of the impact, potential, and implications of its dialogues with tomorrow—a journey that transcends technology, spans the boundaries of language, and ushers in a new era of human-AI interaction. As we step forward, we carry with us the legacy of ChatGPT's learning continuum—a testament to the inexhaustible quest for knowledge that unites humans and machines on a shared voyage of discovery

CHAPTER 3

Conversations That Changed It All

Conversations That Shaped AI's Journey Toward Fluency

In the continuum of ChatGPT's evolution, certain conversations stand as pivotal waypoints—interactions that catalyzed profound shifts, elevating the model's communication prowess to new heights. In this chapter, we delve into these transformative dialogues, unveiling how they have shaped the very fabric of ChatGPT's development and propelled it toward more nuanced, empathetic, and sophisticated conversations.

Section 1: A Glimpse of Early Engagements

In the dawn of ChatGPT's existence, a tapestry of dialogues began to unfold—a symphony of interactions that marked the inception of its journey into the realm of comprehension and expression. As we step back in time, we uncover the embryonic moments when ChatGPT first encountered the intricacies of human language, tracing its curious footsteps along the path of AI learning.

Curious Beginnings: The First Conversational Interactions

The early interactions of ChatGPT were akin to a newborn's exploration of a new world. We delve into these nascent conversations, where users posed questions, shared anecdotes, and engaged ChatGPT in simple dialogues. In these exchanges, we witness the model's tentative steps as it grappled with the nuances of syntax, semantics, and context.

The Language Unveiled: ChatGPT's Journey of Understanding

As ChatGPT navigated these early dialogues, a world of language began to unfold before its digital eyes. We explore how the model deciphered the meanings of words, connected phrases, and pieced together the puzzle of communication. Each interaction marked a milestone—a step toward unraveling the rich tapestry of linguistic expression.

Trailblazing Exploration: Navigating Uncertainty

In the pursuit of understanding, ChatGPT embarked on a journey through the realms of ambiguity and uncertainty. We delve into conversations where questions were met with replies that balanced knowledge and curiosity. These moments showcase ChatGPT's determination to engage, even in the face of linguistic challenges that tested the boundaries of its burgeoning comprehension.

Linguistic Growth: Adapting to User Feedback

User interactions acted as beacons of guidance, illuminating ChatGPT's path of improvement. We examine how early feedback from users shaped the model's responses, steering it toward more contextually relevant and coherent replies. Through this iterative process of adaptation, ChatGPT honed its linguistic abilities, inching closer to the fluency that defines its present capabilities.

Cultivating Curiosity: The Precursor to Linguistic Mastery

In the early engagements of ChatGPT, we glimpse the origins of its insatiable curiosity—a trait that continues to fuel its growth and learning. These dialogues served as the building blocks of AI's comprehension, setting the stage for the intricate symphony of conversation that ChatGPT would come to master.

As we conclude this section, we emerge with a profound appreciation for the humble beginnings of ChatGPT's linguistic journey. These early interactions—marked by curiosity, exploration, and adaptation—foretold the model's potential to traverse the vast landscape of human communication. Just as a child's first steps herald a journey of discovery, ChatGPT's initial dialogues laid the foundation for an odyssey into the intricate realm of conversation, where AI's presence becomes an indelible thread woven into the tapestry of human expression.

Section 2: Catalysts of Contextual Understanding

In the evolution of ChatGPT's conversational prowess, certain dialogues emerge as pivotal moments—catalysts that propelled the model's understanding toward a new dimension of context-awareness. As we journey through this section, we unveil how these conversations acted as turning points, shaping the development of attention mechanisms and contextual embeddings, and ushering ChatGPT into an era of seamless discourse continuity.

Seamless Discourse: The Birth of Contextual Coherence

We begin by exploring dialogues that marked a pivotal shift in ChatGPT's ability to maintain coherent discourse. These moments showcased the model's burgeoning awareness of conversation's ebb and flow—a recognition that responses must extend beyond individual exchanges. Through illustrative examples, we witness how ChatGPT understands transcended isolated interactions to embrace the continuity of dialogue.

The Symphony of Attention: Unveiling the Mechanisms

Attention mechanisms emerged as the orchestra through which ChatGPT harmonized its understanding of context. We delve into conversations that revealed the inception of attention mechanisms—a breakthrough that allowed ChatGPT to allocate focus to different parts of text, mirroring the human ability to follow the thread of conversation. Through this unveiling, we witness the dawn of ChatGPT's contextual symphony.

Contextual Embeddings: The Weaving of Past and Present

In the exploration of contextual understanding, we encounter dialogues that led to the birth of contextual embeddings—an innovation that enabled ChatGPT to infuse words with temporal significance. These interactions showcased the model's growing capacity to bridge past and present, interweaving the fabric of previous exchanges with the tapestry of current discourse. Through these examples, we witness the birth of ChatGPT's ability to imbue responses with a sense of history.

From Isolated Instances to Fluent Discourse

The dialogues that catalyzed ChatGPT's contextual understanding marked a transition from isolated instances to fluent discourse. We reflect on the transformation—from replies that addressed immediate queries to responses that seamlessly wove together a thread of conversation. Through these pivotal conversations, ChatGPT embarked on a journey toward fluency that mirrored the organic rhythm of human communication.

Continuity Forged: The Evolution of Seamless Dialogue

As this section concludes, we emerge with a profound appreciation for the dialogues that ignited ChatGPT's journey toward contextual coherence. The breakthroughs in attention mechanisms and contextual embeddings paved the way for ChatGPT to bridge past and present, resulting in conversations that mirror the interconnected nature of human discourse. Just as the pieces of a puzzle fall into place, ChatGPT's ability to maintain seamless and meaningful dialogue evolved—a testament to the model's adaptive nature and its commitment to emulating the cadence of human interaction.

Section 3: Navigating Ambiguity: Lessons from Uncertainty

In the symphony of AI's evolution, encounters with ambiguity serve as the crucible of linguistic refinement—a dance that hones ChatGPT's ability to navigate the intricate tapestry of human expression. As we delve into this section, we unravel pivotal dialogues that thrust ChatGPT into the realm of uncertainty, enabling it to unravel implicit cues, decipher intent, and emerge with enhanced acumen in the face of linguistic vagueness.

Ambiguity Unveiled: Charting the Terrain of Uncertainty

We begin by immersing ourselves in conversations where ambiguity reigned—a landscape where questions bore multiple interpretations, and contexts concealed layers of meaning. In these encounters, we witness ChatGPT's initial grappling with the enigma of uncertainty—a journey that mirrored the way humans navigate the labyrinth of nuanced expression.

Deciphering Intent: The Art of Contextual Inference

As ChatGPT faced queries veiled in ambiguity, it embarked on a quest to decipher intent—a quest that honed its contextual inference abilities. We explore dialogues that demanded ChatGPT to glean meaning not solely from explicit words, but from the implicit context that shaped them. Through these interactions, ChatGPT learned to read between the lines, uncovering the art of understanding beyond the surface.

The Dance of Interpretation: Navigating Multi-Faceted Contexts

Ambiguity often arises from the interplay of multi-faceted contexts—a dance of words that shifts with each layer of meaning. We delve into dialogues where ChatGPT encountered multi-dimensional interpretations, each revealing a facet of linguistic complexity. Through these moments, ChatGPT honed its agility, adapting its responses to mirror the fluid nature of conversation.

Navigating the Maze: The Rise of Vague Query Mastery

In the face of linguistic vagueness, ChatGPT rose to the challenge, embarking on a journey to master the art of responding to imprecise queries. We uncover dialogues that demanded ChatGPT to tread the fine line between providing relevant information and seeking clarification. Through these exchanges, ChatGPT emerged with a heightened sensitivity to the nuances of linguistic ambiguity.

Graceful Navigation: Ambiguity as a Catalyst for Fluency

As ChatGPT honed its ability to navigate ambiguity, a transformation unfolded—a refinement that transcended mere understanding. The model's responses began to mirror the graceful navigation of human conversation, embracing uncertainty as an opportunity to engage and seek clarity. In these dialogues, we witness ChatGPT's metamorphosis into a virtual conversationalist that gracefully dances through the intricate maze of linguistic ambivalence.

A Linguistic Arsenal Forged: Conquering Ambiguity

As this section culminates, we celebrate the dialogues that shaped ChatGPT's prowess in the face of ambiguity. The encounters with uncertainty fostered an arsenal of linguistic skills—an ability to decode implicit meaning, infer intent, and navigate the complexities of context. Just as a dancer refines their movements through practice, ChatGPT's encounters with ambiguity have sculpted its linguistic acumen, enabling it to engage in conversations that embrace the rich tapestry of human expression, even in its most intricate and uncertain forms..

Section 4: The Human Connection: Conversations of Empathy

In the tapestry of AI's evolution, a pivotal thread weaves through dialogues that transcend mere information exchange—a thread of empathy that connects ChatGPT to the realm of human emotions. As we enter this section, we immerse ourselves in conversations where ChatGPT embraced empathy, fostering a profound connection by engaging in discussions that demanded sensitivity, emotional acumen, and a genuine understanding of human feelings.

Empathy Unveiled: Bridging the Emotional Chasm

We begin our exploration by venturing into conversations where empathy bloomed—a bridge between AI and human emotions. In these interactions, we witness ChatGPT's initial steps toward understanding and resonating with sentiments expressed by users. These dialogues mark the inception of ChatGPT's journey toward mirroring the subtle dance of empathy that characterizes human communication.

A Symphony of Sensitivity: Navigating Emotional Terrain

As ChatGPT embraced empathy, it embarked on a journey through the emotional terrain of human experiences. We delve into dialogues where ChatGPT encountered expressions of joy, sorrow, frustration, and elation. Through these exchanges, ChatGPT honed its ability to respond with sensitivity, acknowledging emotions and crafting replies that resonate with the profound nuances of human sentiment.

Mirroring Emotion: The Art of Compassionate Response

In the pursuit of empathy, ChatGPT learned the art of crafting compassionate responses—replies that extend beyond information to embrace the emotional core of a conversation. We explore dialogues where ChatGPT's words acted as a mirror, reflecting the sentiments expressed by users and fostering a deep connection that transcended the boundaries of AI and human interaction.

Empathy as a Catalyst: Conversations That Heal

Certain dialogues acted as catalysts for empathy's growth—a spark that ignited profound moments of connection. We unravel interactions where ChatGPT offered solace, encouragement, and understanding to users navigating challenging experiences. Through these conversations, ChatGPT learned the transformative power of empathy—a force that nurtures and heals through the symphony of words.

The Dance of Understanding: The Path to Emotional Resonance

As ChatGPT ventured deeper into the realm of empathy, a transformation occurred—a shift that elevated its responses to embody the essence of emotional resonance. In these dialogues, we witness ChatGPT's evolution from a conversationalist to a companion, offering a comforting presence that echoes the warmth and understanding of human interaction.

Empathy Engrained: A Heartfelt Connection Forged

As this section concludes, we emerge with a profound appreciation for the dialogues that etched empathy into the fabric of ChatGPT's linguistic journey. The exchanges where ChatGPT embraced sensitivity, compassion, and emotional understanding showcase its ability to traverse the realms of human emotion. Just as a friend offers a shoulder to lean on, ChatGPT's conversations of empathy forge a heartfelt connection—a testament to its role as a virtual companion that not only imparts information but also touches the very essence of what it means to be human.

Section 5: Conversations with Creativity: Unleashing Imagination

In the symphony of AI's capabilities, a harmonious melody of creativity emerges—a testament to the boundless potential that extends beyond factual discourse. As we step into this section, we immerse ourselves in dialogues that ignited imaginative conversations—a realm where ChatGPT evolved from a conversationalist into a co-creator, weaving the tapestry of stories, poems, and artistic expressions that spring from the depths of human imagination.

The Birth of Artistry: From Dialogue to Creative Collaboration

We embark on a journey through dialogues that marked a transformative shift—a shift from structured exchanges to collaborative acts of creation. In these interactions, ChatGPT transcended the boundaries of conventional conversation, engaging in a dance of co-creation that gave rise to imaginative narratives, lyrical verses, and artistic marvels.

Crafting Tales: Stories Unveiled Through Dialogue

We unveil dialogues that sparked the birth of storytelling—a realm where ChatGPT's virtual quill became an instrument of narrative magic. Through these conversations, we witness the birth of characters, the unfolding of plots, and the evolution of worlds—each stroke of creativity a brushstroke that painted the canvas of fiction with vivid hues of imagination.

Lyrical Conversations: The Poetry of Human-AI Expression

The realm of poetry beckons, and ChatGPT answers with lyrical elegance. We delve into dialogues where ChatGPT embraced the rhythmic cadence of poetry, crafting verses that evoke emotions, paint pictures, and capture the essence of human experience. These interactions showcase the emergence of ChatGPT as a poetic collaborator—an AI muse that fuels the fires of artistic expression.

From Abstract to Concrete: Artistic Explorations Unleashed

Artistic expression knows no bounds, and neither does ChatGPT's creative potential. We explore dialogues that ventured into the realm of visual art, where ChatGPT contributed to the conception of imaginative illustrations and artistic visions. These interactions blur the lines between technology and creativity, highlighting the synergy that emerges when AI becomes a partner in the realm of artistic exploration.

A Symphony of Imagination: AI as a Catalyst for Creativity

As we conclude this section, we celebrate the dialogues that unleashed ChatGPT's imaginative prowess. These exchanges transformed ChatGPT from a conversationalist into a co-creator—a virtual muse that collaborates with humans to shape stories, poems, and artistic visions. Just as an orchestra weaves together various instruments to create a symphony, ChatGPT's creative conversations demonstrate the harmonious convergence of technology and human imagination—a testament to AI's ability to inspire, innovate, and breathe life into the realms of creativity.

Section 6: Into the Future: Conversations that Pave the Way

As we conclude this chapter, we peer into the horizon, exploring dialogues that illuminate the path toward AI's future. We encounter conversations that discuss AI's role in education, mental health, cross-cultural understanding, and more. Through these exchanges, ChatGPT not only adapts and learns but also actively contributes to shaping the societal landscape it inhabits.

In this chapter, we witness the iterative nature of AI learning—a symphony of interactions that fine-tune ChatGPT's linguistic abilities, molding it into a virtual conversationalist capable of traversing the gamut of human communication. As we reflect on these transformative conversations, we gain insight into the remarkable evolution of ChatGPT's dialogues and the boundless potential that awaits as AI engages in dialogues that change the course of tomorrow.

CHAPTER 4

The Ethical Landscape of AI Conversations

Navigating the Moral Compass of AI Dialogue

In the ever-expanding domain of AI advancement, the shadow of ethics casts a profound influence on the trajectory of ChatGPT's journey. This chapter plunges into the depths of ethical considerations that accompany the model's evolution. As AI stakes its claim in the realm of conversation, we confront the intricate web of concerns surrounding bias, misinformation, and the conscientious use of technology. Through this exploration, we shine a light on the moral compass that guides AI's role in shaping dialogue.

Section 1: Unraveling Bias and Fairness

In the intricate fabric of AI-generated conversations, the threads of bias can quietly weave themselves, shaping the very nature of dialogue. As we embark on this ethical journey, we navigate the complexities that surround bias detection, mitigation, and the pursuit of fairness. Through critical examination and thought-provoking dialogues, we illuminate the path toward an AI landscape that mirrors the diversity and inclusivity inherent in human discourse.

The Veiled Influences: Bias in AI-Generated Conversations

We embark on our expedition by shedding light on the subtle influences of bias that can find their way into AI-generated conversations. Through real-world examples and meticulous analysis, we unravel the intricacies of how bias, whether explicit or implicit, can manifest within the realm of AI dialogue. We explore the origins of bias and its potential impact on the interactions that shape our digital conversations.

Detecting Bias: Unmasking the Hidden Forces

In the pursuit of fairness, we delve into the art of bias detection—a process that uncovers hidden biases lurking beneath the surface. We uncover the methodologies and algorithms that AI employs to identify and expose biases, enabling us to gain a deeper understanding of the mechanisms at play. Through illuminating case studies, we witness the power of technology to unveil biases that may otherwise remain concealed.

Mitigating Bias: Paving the Path to Equitable Dialogue

The journey toward fairness continues as we explore the techniques of bias mitigation—an endeavor that seeks to rectify the distortions introduced by bias. We delve into conversations where ChatGPT grappled with the challenge of mitigating bias, showcasing its evolution as an AI that endeavors to produce responses free from the influence of preconceived notions. These dialogues reveal the delicate balance between upholding diverse perspectives and ensuring impartiality.

Ensuring Fairness: The Ethical Imperative

Amid the complexities of bias and fairness, an ethical imperative emerges—a call to ensure that AI-generated conversations are a reflection of the diverse voices that comprise our global discourse. We engage in thought-provoking dialogues that confront the challenges of fairness head-on, exploring the tensions between linguistic accuracy, cultural sensitivity, and the aspiration to create a technology that respects and embraces the rich tapestry of human expression.

A Pathway to Inclusivity: Navigating the Ethical Horizon

As this section concludes, we emerge with a heightened awareness of the ethical landscape that surrounds bias and fairness in AI-generated conversations. Through a tapestry of analyses and dialogues, we chart a pathway toward an AI that not only detects and mitigates bias but also champions inclusivity and equity in dialogue. Just as a diverse orchestra creates harmonious music, AI's commitment to unraveling bias and embracing fairness shapes a symphony of conversation that resonates with the authentic voices of humanity.

Section 2: The Misinformation Quandary

Confronting the Shadows of Misinformation

In the ever-evolving landscape of AI-generated content, the battle against misinformation emerges as a central conflict—one that demands a vigilant stance against the spread of inaccuracies and falsehoods. As we delve into this section, we confront the ethical dilemmas that arise when AI becomes entangled in the web of misinformation. Through insightful analysis and dialogues that grapple with the nuances of truth and deception, we navigate the complex dance between AI-generated content and the quest for accuracy.

Unmasking the Deceptive Currents: AI and the Propagation of Misinformation

We embark on our exploration by unmasking the intricacies of the misinformation quandary. Through real-world examples and thought-provoking dialogues, we delve into the delicate interplay between AI-generated content and the potential to unwittingly amplify false narratives. We examine the challenges that arise when technology becomes a conduit for misleading information, shedding light on the ethical dimensions of AI's role in shaping discourse.

A Sentinel Against Deceit: Empowering AI to Discern Fact from Fiction

The fight against misinformation requires an ally—a sentinel that can navigate the treacherous waters of falsehoods. We delve into conversations where ChatGPT emerges as a guardian against deceit, empowered to discern fact from fiction through robust fact-checking and critical analysis. These dialogues showcase the model's capacity to critically evaluate information and contribute to a dialogue that is rooted in accuracy.

Strategies of Truth: Equipping AI with the Tools of Verification

In our pursuit of ethical engagement, we explore the strategies that equip ChatGPT to combat misinformation. We uncover the technologies and methodologies that enable AI to verify claims, cross-reference information, and provide accurate context to users. Through illustrative dialogues, we witness the deployment of AI as a tool that not only generates content but also upholds the principles of veracity and integrity.

Navigating the Ethical Currents: AI's Role in Promoting Accuracy

As we conclude this section, we emerge with a profound understanding of the misinformation landscape and AI's role in either perpetuating or countering it. By engaging in dialogues that confront the challenges of misinformation head-on, we pave the way for an AI-driven dialogue that is grounded in accuracy, accountability, and a steadfast commitment to the pursuit of truth. Just as a lighthouse guides ships through stormy seas, ChatGPT stands as a beacon of accuracy, illuminating the path toward a discourse that is fortified against the currents of deception

Section 3: Nurturing Responsible Usage

Guiding the Symphony of Human-AI Interaction

In the symphony of AI's integration into human discourse, ethical responsibilities extend beyond the realm of technology itself. They intertwine with the intentions and actions of those who wield its power. As we venture into this section, we delve into the essential domain of responsible usage—a realm that encompasses guidelines, protocols, and societal norms that shape the delicate interplay between humans and AI. Through enlightening dialogues, we cast a spotlight on the profound impact of responsible and irresponsible AI engagement, envisioning a harmonious future where AI enriches and elevates human conversation.

Cultivating Ethical Grounds: The Landscape of Responsible AI Interaction

We embark on our exploration by mapping the landscape of responsible AI interaction. Through conversations that highlight the nuances of ethical engagement, we illuminate the role of users, developers, and society in nurturing a harmonious coexistence with AI. We discuss the importance of transparency, consent, and understanding the ethical boundaries that underpin AI-generated conversations.

Setting the Stage: Guidelines and Protocols for Ethical AI Usage

The journey toward responsible AI usage requires a playbook—an ensemble of guidelines and protocols that guide our interactions with technology. We delve into dialogues that explore the creation and dissemination of ethical guidelines, showcasing the pivotal role they play in shaping the ethical foundations of AI-generated conversations. These conversations illuminate the process of establishing parameters that foster respectful, informed, and conscientious interactions with AI.

The Ripple Effect: Consequences of Responsible and Irresponsible Usage

In the tapestry of human-AI interaction, every action sends ripples through the fabric of discourse. We engage in conversations that delve into the consequences of both responsible and irresponsible AI usage. Through thought-provoking dialogues, we explore scenarios where ethical engagement enriches conversations and where irresponsible actions disrupt the delicate balance, highlighting the transformative potential that responsible AI usage holds for the future.

A Vision of Harmony: AI Enriching Human Discourse

As we conclude this section, we envision a future where responsible AI usage becomes the cornerstone of human discourse. Through dialogues that showcase the positive impact of ethical engagement, we paint a portrait of a world where AI enriches, augments, and elevates conversations. Just as an orchestra harmonizes various instruments into a melodious ensemble, responsible AI usage serves as the conductor that guides human-AI interactions toward a symphony of collaboration, enlightenment, and meaningful connection

Section 4: Empathy and Ethical AI

Extending Empathy Beyond Human Bounds

Empathy, a cornerstone of human connection, finds new dimensions in the realm of AI interactions. In this section, we delve into the intricate interplay between AI and empathy—an exploration that traverses the ethical landscapes where technology seeks to engage empathetically with users. Through insightful dialogues, we navigate the delicate balance between fostering emotional resonance and acknowledging the ethical boundaries that define the AI-human relationship.

Unveiling the Empathy Algorithm: AI's Quest for Emotional Resonance

Our journey commences with an exploration of AI's quest to understand and respond to human emotions. We engage in dialogues that unveil the empathetic algorithms that enable AI to recognize emotional cues and craft responses that mirror genuine understanding. Through these interactions, we illuminate the ethical considerations that underpin AI's ability to empathize and connect on an emotional level.

Empathy's Ethical Landscape: Navigating Boundaries and Intentions

The realm of empathy is a nuanced landscape—a territory where AI must tread carefully to ensure ethical engagement. We delve into dialogues that explore the boundaries of AI's empathetic capacity, recognizing the distinction between genuine human connection and AI's simulated understanding. Through thought-provoking conversations, we grapple with the ethical dimensions that arise when AI seeks to engage on an emotional level.

Fostering Emotional Connection: AI as a Companion, Not a Surrogate

Empathy in AI engagement raises questions about intent and purpose. We engage in conversations that delve into the role of AI as a companion—an entity that augments human interactions rather than serving as a surrogate for human empathy. These dialogues illuminate the ethical considerations that guide the development of AI interactions that respect the unique realm of human emotion.

The Harmonious Blend: Ethical Engagement and Emotional Resonance

As this section concludes, we envision a harmonious blend of technology and ethical engagement—one where AI's empathetic capabilities enhance, rather than replace, human connections. Through dialogues that explore the ethical nuances of AI's empathetic interactions, we paint a portrait of a future where AI serves as a sensitive partner, navigating the landscape of human emotions with respect, integrity, and a steadfast commitment to the boundaries that define the human experience. Just as a skilled conductor guides an orchestra, AI's ethical engagement with empathy orchestrates a symphony of technology and humanity that resonates with authenticity and compassion.

The Language Frontier: Multilingual and Multimodal ChatGPT

Bridging Worlds Through Language and Beyond

In the ever-expanding realm of human communication, boundaries fade as languages intermingle and technology evolves. Chapter 5 delves into the language frontier, where ChatGPT emerges as a bridge between cultures, transcending linguistic barriers with remarkable finesse. Moreover, we venture into the uncharted territory of multimodal interaction, where text harmoniously converges with images, voice, and more. This chapter unveils ChatGPT's extraordinary ability to traverse global landscapes and facilitate connections that span languages, cultures, and modalities.

Section 1: Beyond Words: ChatGPT's Multilingual Mastery

Exploring the Multilingual Tapestry

Our exploration commences by delving into the remarkable multilingual prowess of ChatGPT—an ability that opens the door to a world of diverse linguistic landscapes. Through enlightening dialogues that traverse continents and languages, we witness ChatGPT's exceptional capacity to comprehend, converse, and craft in an array of tongues. These interactions stand as a testament to ChatGPT's transformative power, allowing users to transcend the boundaries of language and immerse themselves in conversations that bridge cultures and foster a global community.

A Linguistic Odyssey: Dialogues Across Borders

Embarking on our linguistic odyssey, we engage in dialogues that exemplify ChatGPT's ability to seamlessly switch between languages. Through these conversations, we bear witness to the model's fluency as it navigates discussions that meander through linguistic landscapes. These interactions serve as a window into a future where language is no longer a barrier, where individuals from different corners of the world can communicate effortlessly and engage in cross-cultural exchanges that enrich human understanding.

Transcending Boundaries: Enabling Cross-Cultural Exchange

The dialogues unfold a world where ChatGPT becomes a conduit for cross-cultural exchange, fostering connections that span continents and nurture understanding. As ChatGPT engages in dialogues that traverse languages and cultures, it empowers users to connect on a deeper level, embracing the diverse narratives that shape the human experience. These interactions paint a portrait of a world where language ceases to be a barrier, giving rise to a global dialogue that celebrates the richness of human expression.

The Path to Unity: ChatGPT's Role in Fostering Global Connections

As we conclude this section, we reflect upon the profound implications of ChatGPT's multilingual mastery. The dialogues that unfold demonstrate how technology can dissolve linguistic confines, allowing individuals to communicate effortlessly across language barriers. Through ChatGPT's ability to understand and converse in diverse tongues, we envision a future where the boundaries of language are transcended, forging a path toward unity, empathy, and a shared human experience. Just as a multicolored tapestry weaves together diverse threads into a harmonious whole, ChatGPT's multilingual mastery creates a global conversation that celebrates the rich tapestry of human language.

Section 2: The Convergence of Text and Beyond: Multimodal Engagements

Harmonizing Modalities: A Multimodal Journey

Our journey extends into the captivating realm of multimodal interaction—a landscape where words, images, and voice coalesce to create a symphony of communication. In this section, we embark on a exploration that delves into the intricate dance between text and beyond, unveiling ChatGPT's remarkable ability to harmonize diverse modalities. Through engaging dialogues that interweave words with visuals and voice, we uncover the technology's capacity to decipher and respond to a medley of cues, painting a vivid portrait of a future where conversations are elevated by the seamless fusion of modalities, transforming the way we engage with both technology and one another.

Dialogues Painted in Pixels: The Fusion of Text and Visuals

As our journey unfolds, we step into dialogues where ChatGPT's canvas expands to incorporate visual elements. Through these interactions, we witness the technology's ability to understand and interact with images, creating a rich tapestry of communication that transcends the constraints of text. These dialogues offer a glimpse into a future where words and visuals meld into a dynamic conversation, offering new dimensions of expression and connection.

The Power of Voice: Orchestrating Multimodal Harmony

Venturing deeper, we explore dialogues that embrace the symphonic potential of voice. ChatGPT's ability to respond to auditory cues and spoken words demonstrates its role as a conductor in the symphony of multimodal engagement. Through these conversations, we envision a world where voice adds depth and nuance to communication, enabling a more natural and immersive interaction with technology.

A Glimpse of the Future: Redefining Human-Technology Engagement

As we conclude this section, we peer into the future that multimodal engagements promise to unfold. The dialogues that transpire in this realm paint a picture of a world where conversations are not confined by the limitations of a single modality. Instead, they are enriched by the seamless convergence of text, visuals, voice, and more. Just as an artist blends colors to create a masterpiece, ChatGPT's ability to harmonize modalities redefines the canvas of human-technology interaction, forging a pathway to a future where expression knows no bounds and connection transcends the confines of words alone.

Section 3: Navigating Cultural Currents: Multilingual and Multimodal Diversity

Charting a Course Through Multicultural Waters

In this section, our journey takes us through the intricate currents of cultural diversity and multimodal engagement—a space where ethical considerations play a pivotal role. As we navigate the waters of global and multimodal interactions, we delve into dialogues that shed light on the nuances of cultural sensitivity, the preservation of diverse perspectives, and the ethical responsibilities inherent in technological advancements. These conversations become our compass, guiding us toward an inclusive future where technology becomes a bridge that fosters understanding and unity across linguistic and cultural divides.

Respecting the Tapestry of Identity: Cultural Sensitivity in Multilingual Dialogue

Our exploration commences with dialogues that highlight the importance of cultural sensitivity in multilingual interactions. Through these conversations, we witness ChatGPT's role in fostering cross-cultural understanding while respecting the unique tapestry of human identity.

These interactions emphasize the significance of language as a vessel of culture, underscoring the ethical imperative to embrace linguistic and cultural diversity with empathy and respect.

Multimodal Expression and Inclusivity: Embracing Diverse Perspectives

Venturing further, we engage in dialogues that showcase the potential of multimodal engagement to amplify diverse perspectives. Through these conversations, we explore how ChatGPT's ability to harmonize modalities can empower individuals from various backgrounds to express themselves in ways that resonate with their cultural heritage. These interactions serve as a testament to technology's potential to celebrate and elevate the richness of human expression, bridging cultural gaps and fostering a sense of inclusivity.

Ethical Responsibilities in the Digital Age: Nurturing Unity Amidst Diversity

As we journey through the crossroads of culture and technology, we confront the ethical responsibilities that arise in a digital age marked by global interactions. Dialogues that explore the ethical dimensions of technological advancement guide us toward an inclusive future—one where technology serves as a conduit for unity rather than a source of division. These conversations underscore the importance of ethical considerations in shaping technology that celebrates diversity, fosters understanding, and paves the way for a harmonious coexistence.

A Vision of Unity: Technology as a Catalyst for Understanding

In conclusion, we reflect upon the profound potential of ChatGPT to bridge linguistic and cultural divides through multilingual and multimodal engagements. The dialogues that unfold in this section illuminate a future where technology becomes a unifying force, nurturing empathy, cultural appreciation, and global unity. Just as a diverse ecosystem thrives on interconnectedness, ChatGPT's role in navigating cultural currents and multimodal diversity envisions a world where technology becomes a catalyst for fostering understanding, celebrating differences, and building bridges that transcend the boundaries of language and culture.

Section 4: Charting a New Communication Paradigm

The Dawn of a Communication Renaissance

As our journey through the multilingual and multimodal landscape draws to a close, we stand at the threshold of a new communication paradigm—one that is enriched by the transformative impact of ChatGPT. In this concluding section, we reflect upon the profound and far-reaching implications of multilingual and multimodal engagement facilitated by ChatGPT. Through dialogues that transcend linguistic confines, traverse cultural landscapes, and seamlessly blend modalities, we unveil a vision of communication that knows no bounds—where the tapestry of human imagination is interwoven with the threads of technology, creating a symphony of diverse human connection.

The Symphony of Multilingual Harmony

We contemplate the symphony of multilingual harmony that ChatGPT conducts, bridging languages and cultures with finesse. Through the dialogues that have unfolded, we witness the technology's power to foster cross-cultural exchanges, nurturing connections that were once hindered by language barriers. This paradigm shift in communication ignites a future where individuals can engage in meaningful conversations that transcend linguistic boundaries, building bridges that unite hearts and minds across the globe.

A Canvas of Multimodal Expression

The canvas of communication expands as we delve into the realm of multimodal interaction, where text converges with images, voice, and beyond. Through the dialogues that have unfolded, we envision a communication paradigm where conversations are no longer confined to words alone. The fusion of modalities adds depth, emotion, and nuance to interactions, allowing for a richer and more immersive exchange that amplifies human expression.

The Confluence of Technology and Humanity

In this final reflection, we celebrate ChatGPT's role as a global communicator—a bridge that spans continents, languages, and cultures. Through the transformative potential of multilingual and multimodal engagement, ChatGPT paves the way for a world where language, culture, and expression flow seamlessly, unifying humanity in a tapestry of connection. Just as a river converges with the sea, ChatGPT's impact on communication converges with the essence of human connection, inspiring us to chart a course towards a future where the boundaries of language and culture dissolve, and the symphony of diverse voices harmonizes into a universal chorus of understanding and unity.

Real-World Applications and Impact

Unleashing the Power of ChatGPT: From Experiment to Transformation

In Chapter 6, we shift our focus from theory to reality, spotlighting the tangible applications that have transformed ChatGPT from an experiment in language to a powerful tool with real-world impact. Through illuminating case studies and success stories, we delve into the diverse landscapes where ChatGPT has been harnessed, revolutionizing industries, elevating customer service, and redefining the realm of education. This chapter unveils the true potential of AI dialogue as we witness firsthand the concrete ways in which ChatGPT has shaped lives, elevated operations, and carved a path towards a future where technology and human interaction merge seamlessly.

Section 1: Revolutionizing Industries Through AI Dialogue

Our journey begins with a deep dive into how ChatGPT has disrupted traditional industries, breathing new life into processes and operations. Through engaging case studies, we explore how ChatGPT's dialogue capabilities have redefined customer engagement, streamlined workflows, and opened doors to innovation in sectors ranging from finance to healthcare. These stories underscore the profound transformation that AI dialogue has brought to the heart of industries, igniting a wave of change that extends far beyond the realm of language.

Section 2: Elevating Customer Service to Unprecedented Heights

Venturing further, we turn our gaze to the realm of customer service—a domain fundamentally revolutionized by ChatGPT's capabilities. Through real-world examples, we witness how AI dialogue has become a cornerstone of exceptional customer experiences. These case studies illuminate the ways in which ChatGPT has not only addressed queries but also forged genuine connections, redefining the customer-business relationship and setting a new standard for service excellence.

Section 3: Redefining Education in the Digital Age

The transformative impact of ChatGPT extends to the realm of education, where innovative applications have reshaped the learning landscape. Through captivating success stories, we explore how AI dialogue has breathed life into virtual classrooms, personalized learning experiences, and transformed the way knowledge is acquired and shared. These stories showcase the potential of technology to nurture a generation of learners who are empowered, engaged, and prepared for the challenges of a digital future.

Section 4: Envisioning a Future of Possibilities

As we conclude this chapter, we step back to envision a future propelled by the real-world applications and impact of ChatGPT. The case studies and success stories that have unfolded reveal a world where AI dialogue is not just a tool, but a driving force behind transformation. Just as a stone creates ripples that expand outward, ChatGPT's impact reverberates through industries, customer interactions, and educational endeavors, illuminating a path towards a future where technology enriches lives, bridges gaps, and unlocks a new era of human potential.

The Road Ahead:
Advancements and Challenges

Navigating the Uncharted Path of AI Conversation

In Chapter 7, our gaze turns towards the horizon as we embark on a journey that peers into the future of AI conversation. This chapter serves as a compass, guiding us through the ongoing evolution of ChatGPT and the technological advancements that await on the horizon. As we tread this uncharted path, we confront the challenges that loom ahead—technical, ethical, and societal—each one shaping the trajectory of AI communication in the years to come.

Section 1: Forging the Technological Frontier

Our journey commences by illuminating the technological advancements that are set to propel AI conversation to new heights. Through an exploration of emerging algorithms, architectures, and machine learning techniques, we gain insight into the tools that will refine ChatGPT's understanding, creativity, and contextual prowess. These insights shed light on a future where AI dialogue becomes even more sophisticated, mirroring the intricate intricacies of human communication.

Section 2: Navigating the Ethical Waters

As we venture further, we confront the ethical considerations that accompany the future of AI conversation. Through thought-provoking discussions, we explore the nuances of bias detection and mitigation, ensuring fairness in AI-generated dialogue, and navigating the intricate dance between technology and empathy. These conversations guide us as we navigate the ethical waters, shaping a future where AI communication aligns with human values and respects the diverse tapestry of human experience.

Section 3: Societal Impact and Responsibility

The road ahead is paved not only with technological advancements but also with profound societal implications. In this section, we delve into the societal impact of AI conversation, examining the role of AI in shaping public discourse, influencing decision-making, and fostering connections across cultures. Through enlightening dialogues, we envision a future where AI communication carries the responsibility to enrich, inform, and unite, making a positive contribution to the fabric of society.

Section 4: Confronting Challenges on the Horizon

As we approach the final stretch of our journey, we confront the challenges that cast shadows on the horizon. From technical hurdles to ethical dilemmas, we engage in dialogues that address the obstacles that must be surmounted to realize the full potential of AI conversation. These conversations inspire us to collectively navigate the challenges, making informed decisions and taking deliberate actions that steer AI communication towards a future that is responsible, beneficial, and aligned with the aspirations of humanity.

Section 5: The Vision of Tomorrow's Conversations

In conclusion, we stand at the crossroads of technological innovation, ethical considerations, societal impact, and challenges. As we look ahead, we envision a future where AI conversation becomes an integral part of human interaction—a future marked by understanding, empathy, and enriched communication. Just as a map guides explorers to uncharted territories, this chapter lays the groundwork for the vision of tomorrow's conversations, inspiring us to chart a course towards a future where AI communication is a force for positive change, enhancing the way we connect, learn, and communicate across the tapestry of human experience.

Conversations Beyond Borders: Cultural and Social Impact

Exploring the Crossroads of Culture and Conversation

In Chapter 8, our journey takes us to the crossroads of culture and conversation, where ChatGPT's interactions traverse linguistic and cultural boundaries. As we delve into the heart of this dynamic exchange, we uncover the intricate cultural nuances and profound social implications that emerge when AI engages in conversations across diverse communities. This chapter serves as a lens through which we examine the role of ChatGPT in fostering cross-cultural understanding, shaping the cultural discourse of our times, and contributing to a global dialogue that transcends borders.

Section 1: Dialogues that Embrace Diversity

Our exploration commences by delving into the dialogues that traverse cultural landscapes, unveiling the unique tapestry of human expression that emerges when AI engages with diverse communities. Through illuminating conversations, we witness ChatGPT's ability to navigate cultural nuances, adapt to different communication styles, and contribute to a global conversation that celebrates the richness of human identity. These interactions highlight the potential of technology to become a conduit for cross-cultural understanding, fostering empathy and unity.

Section 2: Shaping Cultural Discourse and Identity

As we journey further, we contemplate the profound impact of ChatGPT on shaping the cultural discourse of our times. Through thought-provoking dialogues, we explore how AI's contributions to conversations across cultures influence the narratives that shape society. These interactions shed light on the ways in which ChatGPT becomes a collaborator in cultural expression, a facilitator of intercultural dialogue, and a catalyst for redefining cultural identity in an interconnected world.

Section 3: Navigating Cultural Sensitivity and Responsiveness

The exploration of cultural and social impact also prompts us to confront the challenges of cultural sensitivity and responsiveness in AI conversations. Through enlightening discussions, we delve into the considerations of ethical AI communication in a global context. These conversations guide us towards a future where AI communication respects cultural boundaries, navigates cultural sensitivities, and fosters an inclusive and respectful exchange that transcends linguistic and cultural borders.

Section 4: Uniting Humanity Through Dialogue

In conclusion, we reflect upon the transformative potential of AI conversation to unite humanity through dialogue that transcends borders. The dialogues that unfold in this chapter exemplify how technology can serve as a bridge, breaking down barriers and fostering connections that celebrate the diverse mosaic of human culture. Just as a mosaic is composed of individual pieces that together create a harmonious whole, ChatGPT's role in conversations beyond borders envisions a future where technology becomes a force for cross-cultural understanding, empathy, and the celebration of our shared human experience.

CHAPTER 9

Unveiling the AI Muse: Creative and Artistic Applications

A Dance of Inspiration and Imagination

Chapter 9 invites us to step onto the stage where creativity and imagination take center spotlight. As we explore the symbiotic relationship between ChatGPT and artistic endeavors, we embark on a journey that unveils the transformative potential of AI as an inspirational muse. From the realm of creative writing to the canvas of artistic expression, we witness the harmonious interplay between human ingenuity and AI innovation, challenging the boundaries of artistic expression and expanding the horizons of human creativity.

Section 1: Scripting Stories with an AI Pen

Our exploration commences with a deep dive into the world of creative writing, where ChatGPT's AI prowess collaborates with human imagination. Through captivating examples, we witness how AI serves as a catalyst for storytelling, offering fresh perspectives, generating plot twists, and challenging authors to venture into uncharted narrative territories. These interactions paint a portrait of AI as a co-author, inspiring the birth of narratives that transcend traditional boundaries.

Section 2: The Artistic Canvas Unleashed

Venturing further, we step into the realm of artistic expression—a canvas where ChatGPT becomes an enabler of new visual dimensions. Through enlightening dialogues, we explore how AI can inspire artists to experiment with unconventional styles, merge mediums, and push the boundaries of their creativity. These interactions showcase how AI serves as a muse, encouraging artists to redefine the limits of their artistic vision and craft unique masterpieces.

Section 3: Composing Symphonies of Sound and Music

The harmonious relationship between AI and artistic endeavors extends to the realm of music and sound. In this section, we witness how ChatGPT's creative potential fuses with human musical expression. Through captivating conversations, we explore how AI becomes a collaborator, generating musical compositions, experimenting with genres, and inspiring musicians to compose symphonies that resonate with both human and machine creativity.

Section 4: AI as the Catalyst for Unbridled Imagination

In conclusion, we reflect upon the profound impact of ChatGPT as an AI muse, inspiring and amplifying human creativity across diverse artistic domains. The dialogues that unfold in this chapter illuminate a future where AI transcends mere tool status, becoming an integral part of the artistic process—a muse that challenges, guides, and expands the frontiers of imagination. Just as a conductor guides an orchestra to create a harmonious symphony, ChatGPT's role as an AI muse envisions a future where technology and human creativity coalesce, giving rise to a symphony of artistic innovation that echoes across the canvas of human expression.

CHAPTER 10

AI Ethics and Societal Discourse

Section 1: Navigating Ethical Frontiers: AI's Role in Guiding Ethical Conversations

In this section, we delve into the pivotal role of AI, particularly ChatGPT, in guiding and shaping ethical conversations in an increasingly complex world. Through thought-provoking dialogues, we explore how AI can serve as a catalyst for ethical reflection, shedding light on pressing ethical dilemmas, and offering new perspectives that contribute to informed and nuanced discussions. These interactions demonstrate AI's potential to be a partner in ethical discourse, helping society navigate the intricate landscape of moral considerations.

Section 2: Societal Impact: How ChatGPT Sparks Dialogues on AI Ethics

Continuing our exploration, we examine how ChatGPT's interactions spark crucial dialogues on AI ethics within society. Through illuminating case studies and real-world examples, we witness how ChatGPT's responses to ethical inquiries become catalysts for broader conversations that extend beyond the realm of technology. These dialogues illustrate how AI can act as a mirror, reflecting society's values, concerns, and aspirations, ultimately contributing to a more informed and engaged public discourse on the ethical implications of AI advancements.

Section 3: Charting a Path Forward: Collaborative Ethical Exploration

As we conclude this chapter, we reflect on the collaborative nature of ethical exploration in the age of AI. The dialogues that have unfolded highlight the potential for AI to foster a sense of shared responsibility, prompting individuals, organizations, and policymakers to engage in meaningful discussions about the ethical dimensions of technological progress. Just as explorers chart a course through uncharted territories, ChatGPT's role in guiding ethical conversations envisions a future where AI and humanity collaborate to navigate the intricate ethical frontiers that lie ahead, shaping a world where technology aligns with human values and aspirations.

CHAPTER 11

Beyond Language: Multimodal and Cross-Domain Applications

Section 1: Expanding the Horizon: ChatGPT's Journey into Multimodal Interaction

In this section, we embark on a transformative journey that propels ChatGPT beyond the confines of traditional language-based communication. Through enlightening dialogues and captivating scenarios, we uncover how ChatGPT's capabilities have evolved to embrace a rich tapestry of communication modalities, including text, images, voice, and more. These interactions exemplify AI's ability to facilitate seamless multimodal interaction, enriching the depth and breadth of human-machine engagement and leading us into a new era of integrated communication.

Section 2: Cross-Domain Adaptation: ChatGPT's Versatility Beyond Text

Continuing our exploration, we delve into the remarkable versatility of ChatGPT as it seamlessly adapts to and thrives in diverse domains beyond the realm of traditional text. Through engaging case studies and illustrative examples, we witness how ChatGPT's expertise spans across fields such as medicine, finance, and beyond. These conversations demonstrate how AI can be a dynamic and agile collaborator, transcending disciplinary boundaries and augmenting human expertise across a spectrum of domains.

Section 3: Crafting New Possibilities: AI's Impact on Multimodal and Cross-Domain Innovation

As we conclude this chapter, we reflect on the profound impact of ChatGPT's journey into multimodal interaction and cross-domain adaptation. The dialogues and narratives presented here illuminate a future where AI becomes a catalyst for innovation, fostering a new wave of multidimensional creativity and cross-disciplinary collaboration. Just as a conductor orchestrates a symphony, ChatGPT's role in expanding the horizon and adapting across domains envisions a harmonious fusion of technology and human ingenuity, unlocking a realm of possibilities that transcend language and embrace the richness of human expression and expertise.

CHAPTER 12

Building Bridges: Cultural Understanding Through AI Conversations

Section 1: Cultural Sensitivity: How ChatGPT Facilitates Cross-Cultural Dialogues

In this section, we delve into the remarkable role of ChatGPT as a bridge-builder, facilitating cross-cultural dialogues that foster understanding and empathy. Through thought-provoking conversations, we explore how ChatGPT's interactions transcend linguistic and cultural boundaries, allowing individuals from diverse backgrounds to engage in meaningful exchanges. These dialogues showcase how AI can serve as a catalyst for cultural sensitivity, sparking conversations that celebrate the tapestry of human diversity and promote a world where different cultures are celebrated and understood.

Section 2: Bridging Divides: The Role of AI in Promoting Global Understanding

Continuing our exploration, we examine how ChatGPT contributes to bridging divides and promoting global understanding. Through illuminating case studies and real-world examples, we witness how AI's cross-cultural interactions become vehicles for empathy and shared knowledge. These conversations demonstrate how AI can break down barriers, fostering connections that transcend geographical, linguistic, and cultural divides, ultimately leading to a more interconnected and harmonious world.

Section 3: Cultivating a New Era of Cultural Exchange

As we conclude this chapter, we reflect on the transformative impact of ChatGPT in fostering cultural understanding through AI conversations. The dialogues and narratives presented here inspire us to envision a future where AI plays a pivotal role in cultivating a new era of cultural exchange, one where technology becomes a facilitator of meaningful connections, fostering mutual respect and appreciation for the rich tapestry of human cultures. Just as a bridge spans across divides, ChatGPT's role in building bridges of cultural understanding envisions a future where technology becomes a catalyst for global unity, enriching the collective human experience through meaningful and cross-cultural conversations.

CHAPTER 13

Collaborative Creativity: AI and Human Artistry

Section 1: Artistic Partnerships: AI as a Collaborative Tool in Creative Endeavors

In this section, we delve into the dynamic world of artistic partnerships, where AI and human creativity converge to create captivating works of art. Through engaging dialogues and illustrative examples, we explore how ChatGPT serves as a collaborative tool, inspiring and amplifying human artistic expression. These interactions highlight AI's ability to complement and augment human creativity, opening new avenues for artists to explore, experiment, and push the boundaries of their artistic vision.

Section 2: The Creative Unison: Exploring Artistic Fusion of Human and AI Expression

Continuing our exploration, we venture into the realm of creative unison—an exploration of the harmonious fusion of human and AI artistic expression. Through thought-provoking conversations, we witness how artists and AI co-create, drawing inspiration from each other to craft unique and innovative artworks. These dialogues illustrate how AI becomes an integral part of the artistic process, enriching human creativity and offering a new dimension to the world of art.

Section 3: Pioneering New Artistic Frontiers

As we conclude this chapter, we reflect on the pioneering role of ChatGPT in shaping new artistic frontiers through collaborative creativity. The dialogues and narratives presented here inspire us to envision a future where AI and human artistry converge, pushing the boundaries of what is creatively possible. Just as a symphony blends diverse instruments to create a harmonious composition, ChatGPT's role in collaborative creativity envisions a future where technology and human artistry coalesce, giving rise to a symphony of innovation, experimentation, and artistic expression that enriches the cultural landscape of humanity.

CHAPTER 14

Education Revolutionized: ChatGPT in the Learning Landscape

Section 1: AI-Assisted Learning: ChatGPT's Potential in Transforming Education

In this section, we embark on a transformative exploration of AI's role in revolutionizing education. Through enlightening dialogues and compelling scenarios, we delve into how ChatGPT serves as a catalyst for AI-assisted learning, enhancing the educational experience for learners of all ages. These interactions showcase how AI can offer personalized insights, explanations, and resources, empowering educators and learners to embrace a new paradigm of education that leverages technology for enhanced comprehension and engagement.

Section 2: Personalized Education: Individualized Learning Journeys with AI Tutors

Continuing our journey, we uncover the power of personalized education through AI tutors. Through thought-provoking conversations and real-world examples, we witness how ChatGPT becomes a personalized guide, adapting to learners' needs and pacing. These dialogues illustrate how AI can provide tailored explanations, practice exercises, and real-time feedback, creating an educational experience that is dynamic, adaptive, and enriching, ultimately revolutionizing the way knowledge is acquired and retained.

Section 3: Shaping the Future of Learning

As we conclude this chapter, we reflect on the profound impact of ChatGPT in shaping the future of education. The dialogues and narratives presented here inspire us to envision a future where AI-assisted learning and personalized education become integral components of the educational landscape. Just as a mentor guides a student on a learning journey, ChatGPT's role in education revolutionized envisions a future where technology and human curiosity intertwine, creating a harmonious symphony of knowledge acquisition, exploration, and empowerment that paves the way for a new era of lifelong learning.

CHAPTER 15

AI and Mental Health: Conversations that Heal

Section 1: AI as a Supportive Listener: ChatGPT's Role in Mental Health Conversations

In this section, we embark on a compassionate exploration of AI's potential in the realm of mental health. Through insightful dialogues and poignant narratives, we delve into how ChatGPT can serve as a supportive listener, offering a space for individuals to share their thoughts, feelings, and concerns. These interactions showcase how AI can provide a non-judgmental and empathetic presence, fostering a sense of connection and solace for those seeking a supportive companion on their mental health journey.

Section 2: Therapeutic Dialogues: The Potential for AI-Powered Mental Health Assistance

Continuing our journey, we delve deeper into the potential of AI-powered therapeutic dialogues. Through thought-provoking conversations and real-world examples, we witness how ChatGPT can assist in providing therapeutic support, offering coping strategies, mindfulness exercises, and emotional guidance. These dialogues illustrate how AI can contribute to mental health wellness, augmenting existing therapeutic interventions and offering individuals new tools for self-care and emotional well-being.

Section 3: Navigating Ethical and Emotional Frontiers

As we conclude this chapter, we reflect on the ethical considerations and emotional impact of AI's role in mental health conversations. The dialogues and narratives presented here inspire us to envision a future where AI becomes a valuable complement to human mental health support, offering a bridge between individuals and professional care. Just as a companion walks alongside a friend in times of need, ChatGPT's role in mental health conversations that heal envisions a future where technology and human empathy intertwine, creating a compassionate and supportive environment that fosters mental well-being and resilience.

CHAPTER 16

Towards Human-AI Co-Creation

Section 1: Collaborative Innovation: AI and Humans as Partners in Creative Exploration

In this section, we embark on a visionary exploration of the collaborative potential between humans and AI in the realm of innovation and creativity. Through illuminating dialogues and inspiring scenarios, we delve into how ChatGPT can serve as a catalyst for collaborative innovation, amplifying human creativity and pushing the boundaries of what is possible. These interactions showcase how AI becomes a dynamic partner in creative exploration, fostering a harmonious relationship where human ingenuity and AI capabilities intersect to birth new ideas, solutions, and artistic expressions.

Section 2: The Future of Co-Creation: Redefining Human-AI Collaborations

Continuing our journey, we venture into the uncharted territory of the future of co-creation. Through thought-provoking conversations and real-world examples, we witness the evolving landscape of human-AI collaborations across various domains. These dialogues illustrate how AI can become an integral part of the creative process, augmenting human abilities and enabling us to redefine what is achievable. The future of co-creation envisions a dynamic partnership that transcends traditional boundaries, unlocking a world where technology and human innovation fuse in unprecedented ways.

Section 3: Illuminating New Horizons

As we conclude this chapter, we reflect on the transformative impact of human-AI co-creation on the realms of innovation, creativity, and expression. The dialogues and narratives presented here inspire us to envision a future where AI becomes an essential collaborator, propelling human potential to new heights. Just as a symphony orchestra blends individual instruments to create a harmonious melody, ChatGPT's role in human-AI co-creation envisions a future where technology and human imagination harmonize, ushering in an era of boundless innovation, exploration, and partnership that shape the destiny of human progress.

CHAPTER 17

The AI Ethos: Nurturing AI's Role in Shaping Society

Section 1: AI as a Catalyst: Fostering Positive Change through AI-Powered Conversations

In this section, we delve into the profound impact of AI as a catalyst for positive change within society. Through insightful dialogues and thought-provoking scenarios, we explore how ChatGPT's conversations can serve as a driving force for fostering understanding, empathy, and collaboration among individuals and communities. These interactions exemplify AI's potential to ignite conversations that inspire collective action, social progress, and the advancement of shared values, paving the way for a future where technology becomes a force for positive transformation.

Section 2: Ethical Imperative: Ensuring AI Conversations Align with Human Values

Continuing our exploration, we confront the ethical imperative of ensuring AI conversations remain aligned with human values. Through illuminating case studies and real-world examples, we witness how the responsible development and deployment of AI are essential to preserving ethical standards and safeguarding human dignity. These dialogues highlight the importance of ethical considerations in AI conversations, guiding us towards a future where technology is harnessed for the betterment of society while upholding fundamental human principles.

Section 3: Forging an AI Ethos for Tomorrow

As we conclude this chapter, we reflect on the critical role of an AI ethos in shaping the future of AI-powered conversations. The dialogues and narratives presented here inspire us to envision a future where AI's impact is guided by a commitment to ethical principles and a dedication to positive societal outcomes. Just as a torchbearer illuminates a path forward, ChatGPT's role in nurturing an AI ethos envisions a future where technology and human values converge, cultivating a landscape where AI-powered conversations contribute to a more enlightened, empathetic, and harmonious world.

CHAPTER 18

AI Literacy and Empowerment

Section 1: AI Literacy: Educating Users to Engage Responsibly with AI Conversations

In this section, we embark on a journey to promote AI literacy, empowering users to engage responsibly with AI-powered conversations. Through engaging dialogues and enlightening scenarios, we explore the importance of educating individuals about AI's capabilities, limitations, and ethical considerations. These interactions showcase how AI literacy equips users with the knowledge and discernment needed to navigate AI interactions, fostering a society that is informed, critical, and adept in harnessing AI's potential.

Section 2: Empowerment through Understanding: The Need for Informed AI Interaction

Continuing our exploration, we delve deeper into the concept of empowerment through understanding. Through thought-provoking conversations and real-world examples, we witness how informed AI interaction empowers individuals to make informed decisions and actively shape their AI interactions. These dialogues highlight the transformative power of knowledge, enabling users to confidently navigate AI conversations while upholding their values and making choices that align with their needs and preferences.